UNMET

stephanie roberts

UNMET

Poems

BIBLIOASIS
Windsor, Ontario

FIRST EDITION
10 9 8 7 6 5 4 3 2 1

Library and Archives Canada Cataloguing in Publication
Title: Unmet / stephanie roberts.
Names: Roberts, Stephanie, author
Identifiers: Canadiana (print) 20240522117 | Canadiana (ebook) 20240522125
ISBN 9781771966573 (softcover) | ISBN 9781771966580 (EPUB)
Subjects: LCGFT: Poetry.
Classification: LCC PS8635.02273 U56 2025 | DDC C811/.6—dc23

Edited by Vanessa Stauffer
Designed and typeset by Ingrid Paulson

Canada Council for the Arts | Conseil des Arts du Canada

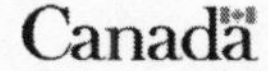

Published with the generous assistance of the Canada Council for the Arts, which last year invested $153 million to bring the arts to Canadians throughout the country, and the financial support of the Government of Canada. Biblioasis also acknowledges the support of the Ontario Arts Council (OAC), an agency of the Government of Ontario, which last year funded 1,709 individual artists and 1,078 organizations in 204 communities across Ontario, for a total of $52.1 million, and the contribution of the Government of Ontario through the Ontario Book Publishing Tax Credit and Ontario Creates.

PRINTED AND BOUND IN CANADA

for Samson James

CONTENTS

I can imagine you, even though I haven't seen you yet.

—Ursula Andkjær Olsen, *Third-Millennium Heart*

I WORRY how low
the bar has been set it floats
melting in magma

CATCH A FALLING KNIFE

Late May, Nova Scotia
tears into flames. Our new normal,
we are told.

Western wildfires bathe British Columbia,
soap its armpits in smoke
and carelessness. At-risk sequoias
hold their breath while men skirt
General Sherman in foil.

I bought in—
Us! and a future
of compound interest. Us! taking
turns setting the table with
steady growth after rain.

Losing trust loses face. Grief
bangs on the counter,
demanding to see the manager.

Financial literacy stands five
nothing. It rubs the knees
of inherited wealth, a basketball team
that gets three points even under
the hoop.

Deep losses coursed down
the back of August, red, all over
us and everyone else;
the bottom rose to meet me
with no rebound in sight.

Eat year-end scarlet rare, a cardinal,
a tanager, the fine mist of high
caliber kiss, year upon year, carry
hits forward. Hold negative print
for a hoped-for Black Friday.

It erased everything in me to see
your absence taken off the books,
each entry an imagined haul
the hell out of here.

MALL OF THE SIRENS

Willows tremble, in from the road,
near water's lip,
where one would wish to be instead of here
dollar store, drumming in line, humming Hendrix,
holding fridge magnets, plastic daises you don't want,
a doodad you'd realize doesn't suit your frame
if you took a beat to let yourself
rise to your own amazement, which is beyond
the atrium's glass ceiling,
beyond the tang of loneliness
in the storm nestled at heart level.
This is what comes of taking dreams
off the horizon. It is the sun
or nothing else, you would scream
if you weren't caught up in the chorus.

An acorn folded its arms.
It desired death in black's riches.
This is also what you wanted
when you first got hold of it.
Chest-pocket-placed wishes grew overly precious
like a tongue covers decay in tooth. Desire, wish,
& will fought like tights in the laundry.
You jumped fences without losing breath.
You could keep the bow toward sunset.
Today felt like all the time in the world. Eyes to sky
small running start with a tree asleep

at your breast. Everything smooth is rose-toned
& false. It was the sun or nothing else
you mumble to nobody. Only sun.
Now you won't reach home. You never
reach home.

LADY FINE IS FOR SUGAR

My grandmother believed in it
delicate laugh perfectly pressed blouse
blouse not shirt and proper grammar
billowing it out

You are well, not fine. Fine is for sugar!

Shorthand typing secretarial position
with some florid-faced boss drew success
my mother stormed like rain
teen pregnancy loud laugh bellicose
swore freely in front of her children

i am the sky that could fall either way

Lady passé and enduring mythology
i feel some sorta way over Cardi B
precisely because she levitated up a stripper pole
like a fuckin' phoenix against the stench
of respectability politics

like a motherfuckin' phoenix through the ceiling
burning on the hydrogen of unwavering respect
bricks of dollar signs gain
plush in the same country where Abuela believed
you had to play the Lady game

Star-spangled fantasy
my mother knew the danger
the voice that can't be heard
the suspect testimony of that pressed blouse
flesh-tone foundation obscures
black and blues
white Peter Pan collar
crossed ankles
the *I'm well, thank you.*

PURE DICTATION: HOW MY DREAMS HAVE FLOWN MOST OF MY LIFE BUT TONIGHT IT ALL MAKES SENSE

i'm wary of

what i'm told

resisting labels—especially
ones people sell

about themselves

on a midnight barstool
toast quickly to the one

shoved off

superposition superman market
size—whimsical words for

much

the older you get the more
you're inured to the absurd

i agree (but not really) roll my eyes
that resignation is virtue

(fuck marcus aurelius)

you pray how you feel doesn't matter
without ceasing
anarchy charges

your despair

the swampland

where a floodplain of

barking monkeys

six feet under
high water mark glistens

people say you can't
read in dreams a myth

i'm taking pure dictation
reading these words

now.

UNMET

we simmer in the shade of sun surround.
begin ending or ripely enjoying middle
in split silence in outdoor-level laughter.

to keep me from writing, to keep that love
from eclipsing this, you make erotic requests
in English in Italian with eye part bulldog part wolf.

true, one afternoon, lava lapping my spine,
I made you put down your Makita
to break your back a little. what goes around.

silence stiffens your neck. we changed address.
we, unsure if lightning cracks a mundane night,
or the common unravels, or is this a tennis match

of recriminations with court as net. could be
all of these. a firetruck wails as only in summer.
you look over your glasses & I slip

shoulder straps over hills down valley.
Marilyn Monroe had this radiation,
nakedness was her tongue of fire.

during services, as a child, she sat
on her hands, bit her lip, & for a minute,
forced a smaller self against the world.

FETTER

I had a pain in my leg from the fetter, and now I feel the pleasure coming
that follows it. —Socrates

You can't tell if he's joking. Is he thankful?
This is not why I ask you to secure me to the headboard. There is no medal
sufficient for suffering though many grit their teeth.

If there were a trigger to explode the face of pain, I would pull it. Even repulsed
(as I am) by gun violence, punishment corporal and capital, the imprisonment
of addicts and every filed tooth of power that proves us more fear than love.

Where was I? Ah yes! (still strapped to the headboard and you over me, and you
over me, trying to mitigate my sins) This private view, no shame, hemmed body
trust not pain.

TO CALL MYSELF

. . . to feel myself beloved on the earth.
—Raymond Carver

A woman frees her home of white dust.
Now light ambers polished mahogany.

What is the point of calling your tapeworm
adoration if that hunger leaves your rage

alone in its oven.

If my light can't scythe the clay legs
from under you then what's the use.

I will will elsewhere; fill another valley;
find spanking new mistakes.

A woman orders rose-shaped pink
pleasure with courage for tomorrow.

During Manhattanhenge I saw myself
mirrored in the Vertical Without You.

Sunrise, oh 42nd! The gold Adhan. I
with the flex of myself loosed

rising to cloud. Shine like gilt winter
birdsong, my alone throat roaring.

UNMET & UNSENT ~~(TO ANOTHER SOUTHERN POET)~~

for Steve

The pressed red leaves are from a shrub I planted.

I keep inside & north
I send paper, paint, leaf
pressing my form
my likeness to shyness
between wax paper where
you may look
but not touch

already twice bitten
barn sour & given to be double
the fool
I fast intermittently
then stand behind double-wide trees
tuck in elbows
fold in my corners
chip off my shoulder
to mail you the bit
placing the rest under
the back door welcome mat

open the envelope
to sigh at small sharps
or hunger for more

ground hog or no ground hog
now we open our windows without
getting our hides snatched off
no worry about anything buzzing in

before Waverly went terminal
when Virginia-high & log cabin off-grid
were a day more than dream
before (within months of each other)
he & his old man
shut the door for good
on the family name
long before mortality
utterly cleared its throat
I asked him to handstitch me a kerchief
in Union Blue calico
it waves goodbye now

thank you for your shadow
in your poem I hear my uncertainty
bleat for any unlocked door
you put the best of yourself
between your lines
& I can't help falling
seeing you as perfect
the way god sees us.

What the arsonist doesn't understand about
herself she incinerates.

—Jeff Alessandrelli, *Fur Not Light*

THE PROCESS

You have written a lot of idiotic things
Under the question of it. What it is
And with how many horns? What
Parts lips and legs? Flippant one day
Evasive the next, you are a fool,
Of gently shrugging shoulders, trying
To tie cats' tails together into certainty.

In an empty apartment, you butter
A sandwich on both sides with daydreams.
A memento dropped in cola
Is desire. You reassemble aftermath
Before the whole unravels.
Acid astringent sweet bitter slurry,
Inviolate chemistry disregarded
At your loss. Now we're baking cake.

Your childhood was stored
In Abuela's basement, an inflatable clown
You punch but can't knock over. Not
The way first love lands one squarely.

Afflicted by the bud-green thrusts
Of March, it's important to weed out hurry.
Slow your heartbeat
Biathlete. Pour two digits of bourbon
Into Grandpappy's highball glass.

With no timekeeper at the finish,
With no Great Baker in the sky,
The waft of vanilla to the next floor
Tells you that you hardly need to touch it.
But softly you touch it, testing for spring-back.
Stick a knife in the centre. It must come out clean
To prevent collapse.

ESTABLISHING AN AIRWAY

After dissecting everyone
and burning their pieces
across the plain of my memory
what will be left?
I who in pressed lip despair
search the town Compassion
where I might lay down scalpel
rib spreader
enucleator
        this   flamethrower
that blazed a bearable path
from my mother's stranglehold
or brought me to a bridge
over an eroding river.

Doctor El-Said's eyelashes above
her mask were black lace curtains
with a voice velvet and relaxing
as a glass of pinot noir.
I am your anesthetist your breath
is in good hands. My elevator operator
of the dreamless dark. The same moment
the doors close the light comes back on
and I am alone with all limbs reattached.

Tenderness,
population: who knows.
If I found a person   like a place
like a lay-down-your-head-against-forever
would they find cup, bowl, spoon
or just the ice that winks
in the base of a bootprint in snow
amid the cyanotic fingers of March
memory only
ghost of the necessary air.

BLACK CONVERSATION

from the noose of the poem
the dead woman points off page.
follow her finger to the blue eyes
of the poet
who caps and uncaps
a black fountain pen.

he looks at her finger, wipes his eyes,
scrolls down, *not I*.

he is sympathetic.

although the purple tongue,
tied shut in its duchess, has a lot it could
say, it wouldn't be saying anything
that hasn't been said before.

her arm maintains indication.

the poet unscrews his pen, marks
the sky—azure, the river—tempestuous,
the bystanders, the good-ole-days,
the rape, the neck, the feet (going
nowhere), the bystanders, the show
not tell.

plus ça change . . .

turn-of-the-century postcard,
the body camera, the hoodie, the bystanders,
the wife beside you, the stanza,
the assonance, the brains-
patterned dashboard, the bystanders,

the line
breaks.

his montblanc outlines
her obsidian necklace in mangled AAVE.
he screws his pen back together
the pushcart is coming.

ONCE AGO YEARS

On Girouard Street one of the prostitutes
took his wife's teal blue boots
that her mother paid full price for at Eaton's.
He asked for them back
at the apartment across the way
before his neighbour pulled a knife
before the knife was better described as machete
before *The Force* would come
for sixteen-year-old Kevin, who lived upstairs
and, as a Black boy, was perilously large
for his own safety, and after that neighbour
pulled that knife, the man's wife
shouted past the chained door into
the hallway chaos of NDG
I have called the police. Back when
she believed that cops could do
any good, back when she didn't know
she was risking her life. Kevin of course
also in that hallway
spoke thru the chink, beyond winks
of steel and all the indifference
to affordable housing that would bring them
to this moment. *That is very nice*
wallpaper. A flat Canadian accent. *You have*
a lovely apartment.

* * *

A man, if this is a man, punched his wife, who
Is definitely his wife, in her face. Nasal blood
Mingled as salty brook. Call this brackish
As her nieces noted the town's tone.
Silence. That not-at-all funny   uncle.

* * *

A woman, an aunt, a mother, abuela
cries in the night; her brown face
a tragedy mask; her nightgown
a nightmare dropcloth for hemoglobin.
I thought, *There is a gun in this house.*
A warning sign flashes lead.

* * *

Imagine a man
Lays hands on a woman
For reasons or no reasons his
Wife or not
I've never heard a very good explanation for what
Men call love

* * *

A poet calls himself a mystic.
I don't know what he means
but it is something certain
literary yt men

call themselves.
This mystic
would not take my *No* for
a no, at the crux of our difference,
tho I wrote that answer several times.
handcuffs Our email trail served as.

* * *

And handcuffs were what The Force
attempted on (too-big-for-his-age)
Kevin for some misdemeanour or
for nothing which is more than enough.
Kevin was saying some indecipherable
yt nonsense about *his rights* when rights
are for judges with witnesses, bailiffs,
and semblances of civility, not for the side
of the road by a police cruiser, or a hall
in an apartment block near the margin,
your rights are what you demand
sitting in court, not from the satin comfort
of a coffin. What I heard clearly was
the screams of his mother teetering
at the apex of sanity. *He's only sixteen!*
Kevin!
Shut up!

* * *

A woman divorces the man
Who once laid hands on her
Once ago years
She answered his question
Mark with the flat of a shoe
To his temple
Exclamation point
A light went on
Like reconciliation
Later moments Many

A woman divorces a man who will
Tread her left garden in steel-toed boots
His sole broke the pale heads off spring
Mashing the hostas erupting like teeth

In passing he cracks off bud-bearing branches
Silky rhododendrons asleep from last summer
A type of abortion   man-caused as usual
No flowers that year or after

***

A husband's heart is drawn
Blind aim to destroy
What she planted
He tells friends
Grew apart They

***

In a poem, she (fucking irate) gestures to maiden-hair fern
gasping under reckless tree stump
a resting place knocked
over.

In a poem, where smile & sneer flicker,
she (considering lesbianism)
gestures to the rhododendron, and
nods to the relative whose blood ran cold
if a certain man walked behind her.   Smile.
Sneer.

***

A cop
On
Camera
Punched a woman
Right
In
The
Face

***

A woman divorces a man
She gone crazy eyeing Ophelia
Lolita, Celie, & terrible Persephone as bachelor
She who will be master'd
She grown hysterical for her PhD

***

Hades trashes hell when he finds her
Gone rethinks the efficacy of his emotion
His mangled messages mixed
Hades
Find the tree that gave in

***

The guy-wires of Hydro Québec passed
through its skin.
The city cut towering cottonwood
to six-foot stump.
Slumped woodpecker rotten & carpenter
ant heavy,
it collapsed cardboard house
on peach blush hemerocallis & narcissus
poeticus hidden in winter.
nose now in the Crushed.

***

Bag the large fallen
Remove by hand the unwanted
Thistle that crept in & rooted
Care for the land she loves
With sausage fingers he tries to become
Himself part of her.

UNMET

Let me tell you about my mourning
then you can tell me about tree planting.
It's that magic season
that hasn't reached you yet.
In shadowed corners
snow stays but already unjacketed
t-shirts breathe like geese like robins.
Monday quiet & empty streets
we will remember spring 2020
with all our suffering.
I had another dream that I was
the confidante of Beyoncé. I woke
under the ocean of it barely saving
myself. Espresso, pinky-tip of honey,
& wanting you beside me.
I was going to get at those taxes
to violate a fine day with drudgery,
but scratch true blue & bird-of-paradise
black. I woke to the picture of you, my lighthouse,
apple tree, ladder, smiling, a radiance like
answered prayer. Shine
in your remote location safe from mask & glove.
My father died yesterday & how on brand,
taking leave in the midst of disaster.
Beyoncé in gold mesh and cornrows, coiled
like a Zambian basket, put a soft hand
on mine. She thanked me and I tried

to pull away. *Oh no!* Something vibrates
in my throat & tears, *You!*
I flush under your sun.

WHERE IS MY HAND ALLOWED TO BE BEAUTY

crown beauty: pastel, bone,
pearl & ivory, unscribed envelope
—never night-handled,
no quarter notes, not sharp nor flat.

where are we in the lyric binders
of beautiful?
where are the inks of our terracotta
& earth fingers against
the annihilating hunger & gnarled
ubiquity of the pale dove's
milk standard?

offer a cup brewed no sugar
no cream to know
more about dark thirst.
are you holding out or in?

our glory needs its own gentle midwife.
its own silk protector against yt poets
who would call it the *n* word, *n*ppy*.

smush the forming kaolin vessel,
most wanted for pedestals, & snatch
at gold ring thieving.

with a mouthful of volcanic beach

I gesture dusky middle finger (slim
& magic) to where I want to be.
is this all allowed me?

THE DOG IN CHARGE OF BOY

The man in charge of rice starves to death, while leaning on the sacks of rice.
—"Pavlovsk Station," Erin Noteboom

You could die on the unshared sack of yourself
but not today my love.

A dog finished in fire curled by the sooty face
of a boy—close fur, wet nose, tiny grant of mercy.

The man in charge of rice refines profession
—paid occupation, declaration of belief.

One day I stood shadowed by a liminal smirk,
his raised eyebrows innocent as a red hand.

One day I part a plate in half
against the guillotine of table's edge.

Dog expires near missed boy, a mother's hunger,
and the scientist against a saved nation. I lean

on my diamond mind refusing an end on vacant
promises. The dog in charge of boy wasn't bound

by law, didn't know what we call love, bound
by neither profession nor profession.

SPIDER KITING

on a single let-out tail of silk
an octet of legs is borne away.

we so alike we are an ocean;
we so alike we're the same polarity.

less falcon-fall, less fire-grabbed,
certainly we fault Icarus.

into a dream, i mouthed *anchor me*,
whispered *cloth*, between our bow of lips.

love the line in your palm,
and feet roots, the spool's secure filagree

of confinement. don't be afraid of the nude
folded future at beautiful hand.

the silver line snagged its aorta on edge
of sky. take me now hand to mouth.

say, in a low voice, *stay*. don't title the loose end:
Inevitable,

or call my solitude, sunbeam-steamed-away,
Fate—not the kiss we're taking.

NOTHING OF THE MONTH CLUB

Wearing a lightweight twill jacket,
a woman walks out the door with her life.
She deposits the key in a snow-coated
storm drain and keeps it moving.

Better the exchange of the hundred thousand
the bank requires for nothing. She goes.

And thinks *ghosting* is alchemic poetry
the invisible comes concrete. For years husband,
family, a lover, have all passed thru her. She pulls
desire by its ears, wriggling, right out of her hat.
She removes nose ring, vermeil necklaces, brace-
lets, anklets and excuses herself from the offer
of a well-picked-over buffet.

Every month let nothing new be delivered me.
Zero, be my centre! If I have learned nothing
from this life, I have learned to be grateful
for what I have not.

On Canal Street, her husband shuffles three cards.
Keep your eye on the queen, he says over and over.

for Jeff Alessandrelli

EINIGE KREISE (SEVERAL CIRCLES)

January–February 1926

I imagine it had to be cold. The exhibit audio
said there was a voice, he got lost in it,
a switchboard operator, had to move her
from dream to memory, have dinner
together that same night.

Several circles may well be
a time of year grounded
on nocturnal skyscape, colour
scumbled, opaque & transparent
comments all of life and breath
in the imagination's ouroboros.

I'm gaining on Kandinsky's completed
circle, yet the robin's song returns.
How do found and lost
have equal weights of permanence?

A thoughtfully arranged bouquet
opens with more & more power before
it glows over, and even if we didn't photograph
every sneeze, the breeze of blooms echoes

mother to son the baby who would not nap
falls asleep at the wheel on his way home.

It was cold in Munich. Had to be.
Love waits at the end of line;
mind seizes line, draws it
end to end, kisses it to canvas.

WHEN HAROLD OFFERS A FIST BUMP

I stare. May 2020, on top of everything
the cool takes a rise for Kalahari desert.

I shower three times a day, and at night
bounce sexual fantasies about air-conditioner
installers off the ceiling.

When the heat is remedied by rain
no Cinco de Mayo is great enough.

We finally got together a year late
between waves and pre-vaccine. I break
lockdown without knowing what to do
with my hands anymore. Forget lips.
No two-cheek kiss. Now a pseudo bow,
not at waist but a little bit more than nod.

Mad chirps and neon brights feather
a backyard biome. Outside our interiors we
talk poetry and past relationship bullshit.
My neighbours on their *Balconville* fake-
drunk singing like kids who curse for attention.

I can't remember what absolute agreement
drives his extended fist. It emerges
like a train, in slow motion, on a track
I am tied to. How to look away? How

do we manage not to keep wrecking
everything? A moment the brain
refuses to provide the correct French word
at the correct French moment; it can't
knit a hand grenade into
a reasonable story. South of us
they had yet to slalom into the madness
of the later part of the year, when they
hit half a million with a slight shrug
from inside a body bag.

We get up
from the tables of our lives so abruptly
we knock over the chair behind us.

Who was the last man I touched?
What risk was right?

for Harold Hoefle

HOW FAST A HUMMINGBIRD'S WING

i fish the morning salute
above trim of boxers
holding you (cock & moment)
rigid with grace
one's mind scratches
for solution
an armpit of paradox
to a bright mystery of how.

how

any live thing beats
fifty times per second
how the heart collapses
against a vow
that can't contain it
how hard soft can be.

in a cyclone
snapshot occurrence
you hold without holding
let go without letting
go.

i rush
to pin
our happiest together
to the top
of the timeline
of my
surrender.

(butterfly boutonniere tail)

CROSS WORDS

spring swells abruptly in vaudreuil
leaf
flower and scent

he
he   the coming shadow
triangled at my heel while

the outaouais undressed her flanks
fled her bed
came to town nude curious

(what fuss) said the disappearing
shore
what hid in backyard
basements
along st. charles
boulevard

* * *

i sowed myself on high ground
watching

what choices i was making
what decisions had i signed
the way i say to the cabbie

(take me to the adoration mall)

where i sit in a toonie-fed massage chair
for one hour
watching bloated white wrinkles
go by

holiness or sin-ridden avoidance

i'm bone alone though gold

***

it stops raining

the river returns to work

***

jamaica crackles like pork rinds
in my dreams

the issue of he
bronzed he
lingers
aches
        like appendicitis
tingles
poisons aware

fevers winter
dreams wined-tongues
bucking hard in daisied-glades
sweet with mown loneliness
post-expressionist light
strafing our sides
& what's in our minds
nothing at hand unrequited
there is no one unmet

there is

this other
exhausted by his mirror
who brought me along
for the not trying
company to colour-blind
desire
bum-shaped rut
terrified
of failure
my destiny is
night's silver satellite
orbiting after
i slip out of him

panama knits night & day

where's he that clouds me

quiet older giving
sterling depth
                    i can reflect off
burning (as st. paul cautioned)
we are toward under
angry with ecstasy of the citrus-scenting
sun
waiting for each other to dock

* * *

the outaouais returns
dressing in emerald
floor-length
chiffon fate

nova scotia was pulling
the ocean—making butter
full of stars that said

(knife your shine into me)
i've solved the cross
word of your hopes
i'm already thinking of you as darling.

FROM THE TOP OF THE LADDER

He grunts as he scores the sheetrock
that bulges with the hunger of the small
anxious leak in the upstairs bath.

If you drip a drop of water here . . .

He moves her to the crevice of wall and tiled floor,
If you drip a drop here, every second,
it will take a while
(points edge of metal scraper)
but eventually it will run in the basement
(finger down along vertical)
just as fast as it drips up here.

The pinky of his left hand is a fish hook
as he strokes putty knife over ceiling wound.
He bears a semblance to the actor Bradley Cooper
with a shared glacial gaze
and way of talking with a smile hanging on.

With heavy Québécois accent,
and prone to forgetting English words,
(la pelle à poussière?)
(Your dustpan?)
he was born in Waco

only coming here as a teen.
The St. Lawrence sowed a fleur-de-lys
in his bowels and watered it well.

Only a whiff of cigarette stink apart,
he continues, their eyes lashed level,
mouths even above basement drip.

SOUP

After I whet
my mother's thirsty
cleaver
back and forth
back and forth
back and forth back
against stone. I
sing.

Oh Mama, I will section this man.

A plastic wrapped package
is marked *rôti de palette DÉSOSSÉ,*
yes, he was boneless. Cut into cubes &
cornstarch-tossed the flesh gets
whitewashed before the peanut oil's sizzle.
I braced myself against the stove &
chased the dancing with stiff acacia spoon.

At the greeting of iron and rage,
a pot roils, on St. Denis a bicyclist
carries a letter for her father to the post.
She doesn't know he has expired
forever at ease in a bathroom in Opa-Locka.

Done, I say to hope, scraping out quizzical
seared meat and caramelized memory.

Peel thick carrots
and the phantom of fingertips
from my throat, skin
off the trace of tongue
to breast as washed *navets*,
scoop a cup of the heart's red puree.
Crush cloves are devoted kisses,
fragrant coriander, anti-inflammatory
turmeric, good-luck-in-the-New-Year
rosemary, fresh garlic for vampires and Scorpios,
evaporated tears to taste. I forget the bitter sprigs
of winter-bitten parsley without ill effect.
Add the emulsifier of the middle child
sandwiched between success & devotion.

Mingle the messages of mirin, sriracha,
golden courage mustered. Chop green beams
to beef the harmony. There his rawness simmers down.

We are chrysalis now; we are liquid
thin sloshing around like a belly
of booze; we are a pocket of dimes &
nickels,

& I am singing

do-re-mi
across my entire range in time to
metallic claps of lid and rim.

Back at the business of stargazing,
it takes years to turn down the boil.
Years we can't shrug tho we wish
the ability very badly when our necks
were not made of iron.

Light filters a clear broth
cupped in night pottery
hunks of meat float every
song drawn-out sadness.
I stand mellow, raw with debridement
but not too proud, not too burned,
not too confused as not to moan
at the first spoon's spoon.

Roots lost their crunch but gained
sweetness by heat leached from
my exposed bone,
made a woman of me. Daddy,
did I say I moaned?

Throw the spoon to straight hell
bowl to lips, eyes arrested
head back and back and back.

I want to be able to tell
what scurries ahead as a snake
licks the air, its split flesh a chaos
gathering the future
the dire promises of flight and flight
then capture.
I wish for the stainless reach
of a snake's tongue
fool and forgetting soup
with a fork in it.

SKIN

turkey gravy cold in its carafe
congealed tarp floats old latte
bookmark for sinking memory

chlorella pools
the stagnant loop of river we
paddled thru on less jaded days

we floated on our backs
scratching mosquito bites
lily pads and water striders kin

gelatinous thin

tread surface semi-terrified
of depth under I come nose to nose
against my own bloated body
and how to let out our stitches
while keeping intestines in
black bear rug lay
blue snake boot kick
wolf wear scarlet-wool hoodie
our goose-fleshed listening

look

a smile doesn't reach the eyes
the good Samaritan's empathy ruins
the attempted leap from a bridge
public posts of devotion or longing
are licked raw by reptilian thirst
chalk outlines paisley the entire floor

being skinned is how we coat love
what we keep trying to pull off.

GEORGE JUNIUS STINNEY, JR.

In the third stanza he exits the poem,
black tears wishbone
ball lightning.

"On reflection," he said, from the bottom
of his sepulchre, small dark brown fingers
stroking a hairless chin,
"I do not think it was
the hate what took my life."
He straightens himself
on his slab of metamorphosed limestone.
It was the:

Cops kill white people all the time

I'm sure there's another side to this story

If you just obey nothing will happen to you

My family came here legally

POC are the establishment now

I'm not racist but

"I reckon the stack and press of all that *not-racist*
eventually crowned that steel and wire diadem
upon my brow Bible at my bottom."

Lord raise cool sponge to the opening of ebony thirst;
extend a pink hand that smiles without teeth.
White crimes of obedience click as silent syntax to
the flat and sharp sentences of death.

Decades without name, no headstone
no footstone, no identity to his rest lest the Samaritans
lynch even his bones after Old Sparky's revered kiss.

In his final stanza he rises red and exonerated
named in the hearts of the fawn born
not as static electricity but as bolt
that strikes open the door.

CHARLES MINGUS MEANS I LOVE YOU

Miles Davis, Dave Brubeck, Buddy Rich, Dizzy Reece, these are the notes of your song. I should have said I love you. Blue Mitchell, Red Garland, Art Pepper, Charlie Parker. Did I ever say how one we are, knit by coincidence? Long before I heard blue sharps hit soft and hard in my sleep, I wrote a story netting your age, eyes, and aggression; side by side, you played your part and I mine. Swinging. Could *imagine* make your birthday and my mother's the same? I found out on the stress of your Italian sonnet counting back from Christmas. I was right while you left like mother gone like Tuesday. Art Blakey, Betty Carter, Chet Baker, Cannonball Adderley. When I asked: Did I ever say…? I meant, I never said because you are superstitious and signs foretell travel east or west whichever way the wind turns the vane's face. Listen, lover, Sarah Vaughan, Lena Horn, Orrin Evans, Art Tatum. I'm no witch but scientist, mathematician, logician where love solves this quadratic to the parabola of you—my infinite peach pie and denominator that divides me. Dexter Gordon, Ornette Coleman, Coleman Hawkins, Thelonius Monk. Mother was Demeter, that made you who? Hello, I try not to think about it. If there was ever a moment to lose love (as the poets say) let it be spring; let there be a poppy field overlooking the fast river. Charles Mingus.

PISTOL WHIP

granite heart—
even so
i
would've
you
for I vain
vein
open.
i
would've yes
to
single hold
on
a minute
i
not
tin
cup
rattled
Yonge Street
1931! i
tender violent
is
restraint—
what you fear
trembles.
drink

i
giant
elixir
anti
i
suffer. no
i deny
your forever
when
you are
waited
for.
you
percussive
exit
stark upender
of
worlds.

WEAR YOU OUT: LETTER TO A SOUTHERN POET

Was it Tuesday we spoke of musical possession and thought that rhetoricals are seances? Hands on *The Table of Question* summons subjectivity—reality often rejected over the savoury soup of delusion we shovel and excrete. Last night arrived, a Ferris-wheel-memory of song turning; its groove wore smooth the imageless dark.

Relief emerges, like mushrooms corrode the dead log of anxiety, to hear that Louise Glück (whom we both respect) grows likewise entwined and resolute in obsession of some melody's peculiar smile. She said (and charmingly so), *It may have been hard on my family.* And, she listens to classical music which I think particularly forceful to wear one out.

I determine (as much as possible) to wrap crazy. Cocoon a rapture of listening under refuge of earphones where two hundred or more dances thicken a custard of dream's fermentation. In similarity! tempered chocolate needs continual stir and heat—in fixed belief.

When the conveyor stops I squeeze vinyl into molds where the centre holds with snap and shine (godwillin'), perfect balance of bitter and sweet, but what a drive until the Jersey Turnpike, until the broke bone knits, *until you forgive yourself the thing you can't forgive yourself, until the beatings of childhood shrug off weary recollection*, until god stifles laughter at hope held in unnerved-damaged hands, until the ransom demands of the poem are met (stop sending me my body parts), until the seizure of amygdala is sated.

Does melody transpose its throes into the worm of our letters? (Glück concluded not necessarily.) A beg, a please, a ring, ring, ring. Rage for water. Rage against aging. Rage against cowards in hair shirts of virtue.

Five o'clock dawn. Epiphany. Floor jumps to meet the coda of glass—sharp and scatter. Could anything be more decisive? Just as, finally and rushed, I arrived at the climax of the longed for. Conclusion, closure is curtain call, sew him up. The gentle and hurting whisper of a door's kiss. A strain of violins fever into a crescendo of something German and merciless; a crow of completion swells and every second thereafter lessens bold impression, fading, but for the bedside mesh of vellum and squid ink, to net the shadow of fire's here-here-now, writ at the edge of our purple embrace.

We are burdened builders, architects to monuments of sound. We butcher sections of meat thru sinew with the overseer's lexicon—the very whips that ripped our god.

I would sell love for the latest edition of *The Roberts Exhaustive Translation of Every Malignant Silence*—the pauses that cancel understanding echoing into themselves with us tautening the reins of our hearts toward chasm.

In the finale, the chorus sustains such heights half the audience wails while others hear-no-evil—that truth that at length will out.

Dearest, Dear, My! Game up and in, the pitcher lets go but what is hurled is not a ball but himself, his father, his grandfather linked unbroken to Africa. The batter (if he intercepts the arrival of all that iron fortitude) negotiates his own transference of indigo movement, blooming red through his body (internal dance known to be prayer), rote inhalation for emptying life, rich or impoverished as it is, by that subtraction.

From my mother's early rest, I carried the ash of her dreams as nutrients for my garden and pressure to be expended. In the case of this morning, bored through with a mania for the tyger of dawn, striped, alien, and awesome in its separation, as to be, yes, a possession and resonate actuality.

UNMET

You love to swim & so do I. I freestyle bare ass with you first and last.

"There is," you say, "something biblical about our nakedness." When I pull a face, you add *sinful* to appease me.

We give thanks before the plate of each other. "In a dream," I say afterward, anxiety thrumming like a hummingbird backing down my trachea, "In a dream, which wrenched me, I saw your smallish eyes; I carved your flesh out of the granite of the past; I took time placing the gaps in your teeth; I wrote us solid on ruled paper—bee to petal nectar, bee to petal nectar. I pulled you through a straw forgetting bitterness seventy times seven. Burning completion."

Always, I am gored by the ox of my confession, trampled under the bull moose of candour, mauled wide by sabre-tooth of trust. Always.

A ripe persimmon rolls off a picnic table onto concrete. I try to lap it up. I try to pull my jaggeds together. I have ruined my life a number of times by wanting. What do I need to learn from gravity?

You kiss tears and foolishness free of my design. "You're an idiot." You say, a throat full on tomorrows. "Sweet idiot."

ENTANGLEMENT

There is another world, in this one.
—Octavio Paz

somewhere off the coast of orange county california,
the grandest animal that has ever lived swims tangled
in a fishing line.

in a parallel universe, khalila, a blue whale, swallows krill
without joy. something in her whispers mississippi, feeds
disenchantment with the ocean and hostility to her mate.

her moby wears crown and envy of all the pods in the low seas.
alarmed by the baseless nature of this disquiet,
unsure of her options, she wanes in despondent drift.

somewhere, an emotionally distant father enjoys
a crab-salad sandwich. he does not wear a wife-beater;
he's armoured in a crisp oxford—white with blue lines.

in ottawa, on the fourth floor, near the rear atrium
of the canadian museum of nature, i sit
in the chamber of a blue whale's heart, weeping.

a distress call sounds on repeat, tugging bone, tearing me apart;
maybe it's khalila or a nameless whale of our own making;
maybe it's the crab man's son.

somewhere in front of a vintage smith corona, my love knits
a poem on the tinkerings of spiders and the freedom of flight.
in him, the word *clutch* nests painfully, a clogged artery.

we spin the same careless speed in opposite directions;
we tunnelled ambivalent barriers that should've kept us apart;
we are leashed in our longing by a mortgage without end.

THIS IS JUST TO SAY I FOUND THE PARSLEY YOU WERE GROWING

I don't know what we're going to do
about all these beautiful little bastards.
I'm happy about the butterfly,
eastern black, parsnip swallowtail,
all formalwear—ebony fitted,
one-button single-breasted, trim
vanilla-cream pudding
button-down, and cornflower blue
silk tie. Look, its origami light as
our tethering to each other.

Black, green, and yellow striped
they are parsley worms. Swallowtail's children.
Angry osmeterium front sixteen legs
hungry for what is mine what I patted
into the sweet dark earth what I watered
from my sweet white clouds. Come, pesticide
world. Come garnished with greed for
the butterfly's identity: flight and metaphoric.

When we say *they* how are they *they*?
Who said let an Australian mum
come with her child to teach our children
but throw the Jamaican's teaching
certificate in the trash. Leave her tear-
stained children in Kingston. Give her

the diaper bag, give the Haitian sister
a mop, her children wear school colours
and do without her in the perilous
heaving of the Americas' tectonic plates.

We stuff our cheeks with cheap lettuce
and landscape Zellers with red and white tulips.
Our *guest labourers* make due on lower
wages with gratitude then fuck the fuck
on off back to Mexico. They sent Jesús back
after only one season for trying to start a union.

for Amy Mitchell

THE REST

We don't yet know what we will be made of
I think I am
approaching sea star or octopus
marine mercurial beaked you are
canine loyal panting at heel.

We don't have many certainties but this I do know
this I've already seen
you
open to me like a thick hardcover
falls a great height
pages rippling
gabble desperate for understanding
yet incomprehensible
I catch you.

A wind ruffles the sides
of passing motorcyclists
in spring chambray and denim
you steer our trajectory
your luck is the red light ahead.

A kind of ache eases off the cracked tooth removed
titanium screw then crown I am
behind you arms around your belly living *tenere* I
a bit tired a bit worked over by

your bundle of hope thrown in my lap
your long-withheld release
precious wonder wrapped
in the poisons of the past.

UNMET

she dips french fries
in mayonnaise
he suppresses a gag
if we were married
I'd divorce you
and remarry you
so I could divorce you

COMEDIAN

I tape a banana to the living room window
that faces the street which is not a busy street
in not exactly a busy town but
it is also not the sidewalk-free pre-paid
cemetery plots of the suburbs. Not busy
but close. And sometimes in checking the mail,
I open the door and come almost nose to nose
with a fellow citizen, and we are both shocked
by our ordinary surprise.

I list my structurally-dubious semi-detached
three-bedroom one-and-a-half bathrooms
finished basement with the addiction of the
chainsmoker next door perfuming the curtains
and the colourful parade of renters across the way
who get stuck in the snow of my unplowed driveway
up to their axles three winters running.
In addition to their perplexity on the usage
of shovels, they are neodymium magnets
to the steel screws who patrol our fair town.
Asking price: a million dollars.

For a million dollars, cars stop on the close
street to take pictures. The realtors ask if I
will be including the banana in the sale and
of course I'm including the banana in the sale!
I don't want to be hungry for attention
my entire Black life? And while I am doling
out acai-blueberry smoothies and slaps on the back
the mail carrier Jean-Marc slips through
the unlocked door of Canada and eats the world's banana.

Bananas are banal the most purchased
single item at Uncle Walton's superstores.
I and the realtors weep because of the onions
in our smoothies while Jean-Marc squats
in a corner awaiting the coming of cops.
I regret nothing, he says, with the smile
of a shotgunned face. *I regret nothing*.

I also regret nothing. And, before they take
him to his coronation, I kiss his belly a sweet
farewell. No regrets. There are plums still in
our kingdoms of ice.

ARE YOU RED HANDED

If later we don't love each other,
remember, Darling, our worm moon,
ruby velvet flutter of guts,
indelicate first flirtation all teeth & talon.

Acquaintance bridged friendship,
friendship's crimson ascent
coiled a torso of barbed defences.
For forgiving, we forgot me.

Hebrew music without tambourines
is like matza ball soup without the matza,
you said, striped like Picasso
and just as bananas.

Up swankass Sherbrooke West, cherry gelato,
held hands & tongues. When I crack silence
you smile without listening. By way of apology
you say all your lone-child childhood you died
for applause brighter than the grey-paned sky.
My rainbow lips bend chords of your name
in mandrill hue. You can't want what wants
back at you.

For the love of eggs, remember breakfast-
promises with adages of bacon in the fry pan.
I wax brash about *forever* forever,

you gleam, *Not real. Rare air.*
I choose the tower of honest
affection and deserve this height from you.

Alligator, when I grow sick of you
(the way these things snake out), it is written
I loved autumn's fallen members
in spite of your perversity, because of mine.

Love Tests Positive

an easy conviction in whatever court. Are you
caught red-handed? Did you lift her up over

yourself? Write some poem, tell twittering gang
I Love Her, absolved with likes. Reread the azure

story of all you're not. Protest cold contempt but
polygraph your mirror. Laugh at magnolia-scented

nonsense. Feelings steeped in blood must run true,
come ravenous arrow rip into desire's barbecued

ribs. Only this. I tossed out a perfectly good
lung to make room for the concert-hall wound

of your ego and today I am sorry this kiss
cuts rough as a razor's blade

would you rather Judas's gentle peg?
Plant yourself against a tremble of evidence.

Accept *habeas corpus.*
Who said none of this for the wicked.

BLUSH

Yt folks think we can't. He brought it on himself
Said because Citizen knew his rights & tried
To insist on the content of his character which
Will be cobbled together, from shadowed slants
Of his past, during her trial after they dig her
Slugs from what remains of his Black matter.

He stated the facts of being stopped
Without cause & I felt at that moment
The way it claws its way up my cheeks.

With hands at 2 and 10 the Citizen
Asked that a supervisor be present.

On Saturday even god put down his Glock to thank
Himself but every day is the creation of man for
The skinfolk. Together officers murmur a type of
Black mass while his dashboard cam records.

I am a licensed gun owner. I have a licensed gun in the trunk & I do not feel safe.

I don't feel safe sung baritone, alto, soprano,
A tenor such that my fair cheeks flare
Hotter than yt men's sins. When the guttural
Bass of the officer's *Get out of the car* drops

The minute Citizen's alphabet goe s - t - u - v -
W - x - y? She pulls her service revolver & marries it
To His temple. And I am humiliated to see
Myself see this as you also have seen. We see
This One & the innumerable ones.
I imagine, in a more kind time, a Bodycam
Museum like our memory of Peace & Justice.

These folks think we can't blush, have less
Lung capacity, that an oximeter works the same
On our fingers, that an algorithm can't discriminate.
But they're wrong. We blush. We blush at all of it.
It starts in the kettle of our bellies and it burns
Like ethanol flames up the tide of Black history.

I want to throw up when ytt says, about the
Phrenology of his magnetic head, *He brought it*
On himself. Deadly embarrassments. You think
You know your rights when you don't know
Your place.

18 November 2020

I TASTE GOOD AND BAD

At the end of a cartoon, one of the characters looks to the camera
And tells us *take courage*, tells us *be vulnerable* with
The ones we love. It comes to this—memento
Mori from a talking banana. I didn't need it to tell you the truth
And what surprise when this sparked happiness can't make you care.
When hurt I learned not to look in your eyes;
If I wanted to make you disappear I said I didn't feel well.
Is the present road a grocery store or a walk through a needled forest?
By August, tho masks are briefly still required,
They remove the minimum-wager, at the door,
And management trusts us to sanitize our carts, our hands.
The man ahead of me walks in without stopping
While I squirt and rub the lubey gel, marvelling at how
It's possible we aren't blanketed in our own screams. I guess
I marvel because I want to participate, right now, add some
Shatner's Captain Kirk, head-thrown-back, fists-pumping-
For-volume, screams. I loved you from genesis to revelations
Which silenced you like snowfall. Christians ponder what person
In their right mind could see god in all the old guy's glory

And not worship? It seemed to them Lucifer was
By every definition criminally insane. We believe
If people could see our entirety they would run in disgust.
If we like surgeons could see our identical spaghetti
Spinal chords and the harms we suffered as children,
They might forgive us our cheats and bigotry.
In a tender and misguided way you euthanized love
Rather than suffer our inevitable parting you were mixing up
Gin and tonic style. The same ethos undergirds our invention
Of Satan the way we spread peanut butter on toast, when
We're starving, an end to the unbearable mystery of living
The meaning of cancer and car crashes which pokes at us
Like the delicate edge between blade and grass, wind and wind,
Content and content, produce and produce, recreate and recreate,
And lead and lead. Yogurt is half-off so I fill my cart,
The neon-pink stickers beckon as if dairy goods on the edge
Of edibility need lipstick. And what says yogurt like pickles?
I burn old journals, manuscripts, and letters, unwilling to relive
A past with its whimsical relevance or obstinate irrelevance. Why

Try to kill the already so unlikely? Why not rather hope
And purchase this absolutely tremendous jar of garlic pickles.
And now, *I Gotta Get Me Some* ™ chocolate syrup, and leave
The infliction of sorrow to god's eager hand. I'm not asking
You to give what you haven't got, like a beaver's dam,
I'm telling you I can make something of unlikely ingredients.
I have somehow done so before and the earth turned
As usual. I am tempted to buy toothpaste.
My hand hovers over the red, white, or blue boxes, and
Spearmint goes in the cart. I was once in a church of surprise
Birthday parties and practical jokes. They were maniacal about it.
One birthday, the pastor's young wife had to go change
Out of her nightgown; it's not right that someone should look
That attractive so unprepared. Youth, its own beauty.
And once that same Beauty filled chocolate cupcakes
With creamy white toothpaste because that was what we were
Doing those days, biting hilariously into all the time in the world.
I go to the self-checkout and scan the boxes of toothpaste,
Scan my points card then place everything back in the cart before
Pushing it all into the ditch by the parking lot. I don't know

What is obvious. I don't know if you can see what I have suffered

To be ready to be me. I understand now how painfully too-good-

To-be-true slices, a papercut to the tongue. It hasn't been easy

For either of us to arrive at my hand in yours. How far we keep

Coming thru zoos of zebras and pandas, misaligned decades,

Madness and marriage to be both at this sentence. Why discount

All this choice as fate? I don't know what's in a fly's mind.

What makes it buzz my head and hands instead of

The maple-syrup-soaked leftovers at the next table. Flies can't care

About which humans are murderous. Only desire. If you let me

Feed you I would fill your mouth with such tart sour sweet minty

Tenderness you wouldn't believe it.

Red Handed
ladders
hand over hand
out of her net, buys a SAQ card,
a farewell
to a fifty-something husband, Empty,
who held it together
for the children.
Guilty of the knowledge
of good and evil
Red rises
to the wild of her life.

MAY PROGRESS

You move over and you move up
avoiding back and down
for dessert.
Mission control or Tower of London
you struggle for a crow's-eye view
of the gate where a bald man tremors
behind a form-fitting flesh-tone mask.
You shuddered when the scarfed
TSA agent patted down your back
then you both laughed
tho you weren't sure why.
I want to laugh now thinking
of it and you standing,
smokes in hand, at the end of our arid
cul-de-sac, mirage of erotic intent.
If we had watches we would not
be looking at the pulse of our wrists
in agony. But I'm wearing
earplugs by a window over the wing.
We the Vaccinated. We who survive
shuffle a deck of thankful phrases.
Our queen, Reason, reigns
thoughtful about kindness
about consideration
while our antennae insist
compassion is good for the economy.
This Dorval air traffic agent is wearing

shorts he knows he has great legs.
Careful getting your carry-on
into the overhead compartment,
it weighs your past.
No one is sitting next to me
and you are sitting next to me.
We stayed home for a year
grabbing two needles as soon as we could
and stitched our runways together. Careful
getting your carry-on down *abjectivity*
shifts. Have I mentioned
compassion is good for the economy?
Alone on this leg to Vancouver
I left my baggage behind.

UNMET: AGAIN

wherever you're going
i am going with you

say . . .
I'm afraid
say . . .
I'm a yam

i don't want to go nowhere
through nothing
with nobody

say
desire wriggles in your bowels
mute tapeworm
munching
chalk, clay, charcoal

tell fear your dreams never
slept not by my hands
it is you who beat
your fist-sized muscle
half to death
—pulled it
over grates & grates
of regret

place newborn faith on a belly
of shared solitude
warm in the sure-coming
sunset
save all your yeses for me

roost yourself in this nest
put blood over the door of the past
inside
the future has eyes
only for you.

for Cas

A LEFT-HANDED SCISSORS FOR PAUL McCARTNEY

The first jolt of thunder in months
lets itself in off the back porch.
Its shadow fills the doorframe,
top of the head, both shoulders, feet,
travelling thru with a fever's totality.

You heard as a child *"M" was for moose*
(ugly horse with antlers). Bullwinkle J. Moose
only twice as large as Rocky thee squirrel
so when experience corrupts innocence
ages after cartoons and early-readers
but before Rumpelstiltskin offers you
a jar of moose meat in Parrsboro, Nova Scotia,
you accept with thanks but can't
eat because of the smell as well as a durable
phobia of botulism and home-canning.
When you knew the beast's true height
you thought *no way* *no way.*

A sovereign moose severed
the glass-cool Vermont lake on the way
to Magog. The view from the autoroute
was non-negotiable for scale.
Boom.
The morning glory trumpets our longing
for jazz resolution, its final blue notes

petering out under the sun's last call.
Press those valves sweet Tío Handel. We rise,
we fall off the wall away from fairytales.
Hopefully.

Goodnight and good morning.
Sleep feeds our dreams back to us
and in the day we try to argue against
reverse peristalsis when we should
let it get on its gruesome business,
the rescue of our imaginations.
Our childhood quivers in a closet
as more than we can remember,
all the cells at birth replaced.
We are removed.
The tiny wound on the baby's ankle
is a big scar on the adult. *Baby*
I am sorry. So sorry. Here is that apology
you've been waiting for.

I want to start a fight with you
this fight, any fight, every fight,
and every flight too. I want
and I want us to put our fists
together—see how many lies
we knock flat. Thunder

is the part of love that can touch
us safely; I mean lightning.

Students of time and weather
rest your heads while you still can.
Romantic propagandas reach
a rolling boil, gas bubbles
of good cops, and certainty
certainty certainty,
the insistence that our hands
are clean, the innocence of forefathers,
our validity in the uteri of others.
Every stone heart or boulder
says my problem with them
is a *you* problem and there isn't
an argument against that argument.
If they don't see a difference
there is no difference.
The moon points a finger
thru the night's open window.
I can't tell which finger but I know
the thumb is not a finger and
the moon isn't going my way.

Where can I find a telephone booth?
an answering machine? a VHS player?

a left-handed scissors for Paul
McCartney?
At the quake to the air's equilibrium
I think crashing plane,
not rain,
zebras, not horses.
A tremendous fucking electric clap
shaves two years clean off my life.
Rain slices thru our invulnerability,
enters the window horizontally (a murmuration).

There is a squirrel in the refrigerator.
I put it there for the screams.
River can't stop herself
every time I move it.
The obsidian beads of this chaos
monster gleams lifelike.
The bathtub, the downstairs sink,
the top-loader, the cereal cabinet,
the fridge again. Her nerves
spring close on her fingers.
She knows it's coming
but can't help herself. If now
you wish to judge me
exit my timeline, block me, *un-whatever*.
Keep your bullshit divinity. Leave

church work to the abattoir.
Help me, I can't help myself.

For months, in my slice of Quebec,
these streets, this room, this sound
goes missing. Usual winter. It unwinds
octobre à avril. Grandma sucks eggs,
we make sencha tea. I am Black, I have
a night cap, noir knit on the outside,
purple silk on the inside
of the entire winter.

One night in March
thunder breaks up the ordinary
as the guillotine blade surely blessed
the French with justice and I hesitate
during a moment that feels like
dying. Is this the flash
before an enduring darkness?
A last kiss before closed eyes?

Sunflowers nod from east to west.
I hope I survive my selfishness.
Selfish, smallpox blankets the Western world.
And hand in hand we walked the edge
of the Grand Canyon, masked,

half-vaccinated. It was not then but
not too long after that I knew
when you let yourself be shaken (Bond martini)
you see your own bare wretchedness.
Hopefully.
You do.

I have a love-hate relationship with
relaxation. I am conflicted over
conflict. Yes, we watch our lives thru
posted-online-eyes! I meme my
moments. LOL. LMFAO. LMFAOOO...
LMFAOOOO.
An invisible line divides
Laughing Tears emoji
and Waterfall Tears emoji.
An inner eye wanders the aisles
of dollar store after dollar store
after dollar store for an inexpensive
repair. I watched a construction conglomerate
pave a parking lot, they put up
a forest of mirrors so we can walk
as imaginary beauty contestants.

Before a finality of fixes, Marilyn said
A smile is the best makeup a girl can wear.

All Mr. Congeniality's answers are ecru
with beige stripes.
Get off the runway and land your life.

I clawed my life out of ice
and the Beauharnois night was strafed with light,
the faucet of the earth turned all the way
open. A boom. A bang
the whole world happens.

THE UNMET

Your obit contains
Beloved of this poet
Moon, I promise you

NOTES

"Mall of the Sirens" was featured in the League of Canadian Poets *Poetry Pause* and will appear in *Without a Doubt* (New York Quarterly Books).

"Lady Fine Is For Sugar" was featured in *The BreakBeat Poets Vol. 4: LatiNext* (Haymarket Books, 2020), #THEBOOKCHAT, August 28, 2020 (@JoelRGarza), and #WeAllGrow AMIGAS (amigas.weallgrowlatina.com), March 21, 2022, for International Poetry Day.

"Unmet" passages referencing Marilyn Monroe stem from her recollections in *My Story*, Marilyn Monroe with Ben Hecht, (Taylor Trade Publishing, 2007)

The epigraph to "Fetter" is from Hugh Tredennick's translation of Plato's *The Last Days of Socrates* (Penguin Books, 1969).

The epigraph to "To Call Myself" is from "Late Fragment" by Raymond Carver, in *A New Path to the Waterfall* (Atlantic Monthly Press, 1994).

Manhattanhenge is an astronomical phenomenon in which, twice a year, the sun aligns with the NYC grid and can be seen rising or setting on the horizon between the buildings. The Adhan is the Islamic call to prayers.

"Black Conversation": AAVE stands for African American Vernacular English.

"Once Ago Years": *terrible Persephone* is from Emily Wilson's translation of *The Odyssey* (W.W. Norton, 2019).

"Where Is My Hand Allowed to Be Beauty" was republished as a *Verse Daily* featured poem for January 22, 2023.

"*EINIGE KREISE* (Several Circles)" won first place in *The Sixty-Four: Best Poets of 2018* (Black Mountain Press, 2019), and was featured in 2022 at nationalpoetrymonth.ca.

"George Junius Stinney, Jr.": Old Sparky is the nickname given to various electric chairs throughout the United States.

"Wear You Out: Letter to a Southern Poet" references an October 27, 2012, Louise Glück interview with *Academy of Achievement*. *The Roberts Exhaustive Translation of Every Malignant Silence* is wholly fictitious, unfortunately.

"This Is Just to Say I Found the Parsley You Were Growing": "guest labourers" is a Canadian term used for migrant workers.

"Comedian" is an ekphrastic work on the Italian artist Maurizio Cattelan's wonderful piece of the same name.

"BLUSH" references The National Memorial for Peace and Justice in Montgomery, Alabama, which memorializes the documented lynchings of thousands of African Americans during the era from enslaving to Jim Crow in the United States.

"I Taste Good and Bad": *I Gotta Get Me Some* ™ chocolate syrup is an invention of the author. *Désolé.*

"Red Handed": (SAQ) *Société des Alcools du Québec* is the organization responsible for the legal distribution of booze in Quebec.

"Unmet: Again": The line *save all your yeses for me* is indebted to D.C. Wojciech's "LOVE POEM," in *The Longest Breath: Lost Notebooks (2005–2015)* (Anvil Tongue Books, 2020).

"A Left-Handed Scissors for Paul McCartney" samples a comment by Diane Seuss from a virtual reading given in November 2021: "Anytime innocence is corrupted by experience, it's a good thing."

"The Unmet" was republished in *Hummingbird Magazine*.

Closing epigraph: Marilyn Monroe, quoted February 22, 1956, in an interview with Elsa Maxwell for *Modern Screen*.

ACKNOWLEDGEMENTS

I acknowledge the support of the Canada Council for the Arts in the creation of this collection. My deepest gratitude to Biblioasis and my editor Vanessa Stauffer, whose attentive reading affirmed my internal clarity of intention and whose insight and belief in these lines filled the finishing with anticipation.

Thanks to The Doll for immeasurable friendship. Thank you to Deidre, Tia Melida, Handel & Cookie, Brenda Roberts, Jennifer Roberts, Quebec Writers' Federation, the lovely Steve Scafidi, Espace de la Diversité, Dentro La Terra & Nicola Dell'Arciprete, my Bookclub Women, Jeff Alessandrelli, Sage Hill Writing Experience, Melanie, Angela, and my lawyer for being there when I really fucking needed her. Thank you David O'Meara and Harold Hoefle, princes among men. Thank you Daniel M.

Thank you, Julia, for all your choices to shine. Thanks to everyone who practices common kindness.

Some of these poems first appeared, sometimes with alteration, in the following publications:

Event Magazine: "Mall of the Sirens," "To Call Myself," "Where is My Hand Allowed to Be Beauty," "The Rest"
L'Éphémère Review: "Spider Kiting," "*EINIGE KREISE* (Several Circles)"
Poetry Magazine: "Lady Fine Is For Sugar"
The Stockholm Review of Literature: "Pure Dictation: This is How My Dreams Have Flown Most of My Life But Tonight it All Makes Sense"
Burning House Press: "Fetter"
Reality Hands: "Establishing an Airway"
Shenandoah: "Black Conversation"
Experiment-O: "The Dog in Charge of Boy," "A Left-Handed Scissors for Paul McCartney"
Arc Poetry Magazine: "Unmet [Let me tell you about my mourning]"
Pedestal Magazine: "Nothing of the Month Club"
Escape Wheel, great weather for MEDIA: "How Fast a Hummingbird's Wing"
Canthius:"Cross Words"
Twyckenham Notes: "George Junius Stinney, Jr."
The New Quarterly:"Charles Mingus Means I Love You"
The Inflectionist Review: "Pistol Whip"

{isacoustic}*: "Wear You Out: Letter to a Southern Poet"
underblong: "Unmet [You love to swim & so do I]"
Atlanta Review: "Entanglement"
These Lands: A Collection of Voices from Black Poets in Canada (The League of Canadian Poets, 2019): "This Is Just to Say I Found the Parsley You Were Growing"
Michigan Quarterly Review: "BLUSH"
The Festival of Literary Diversity (FOLD) festival program (2023): "Unmet: Again"
Haiku Canada Review: "The Unmet"

"I like Arthur very much, and I'm proud to have such a great playwright as my friend. I've had very few friends in my life, as you know."

—Marilyn Monroe, 1956

stephanie roberts is the author of *rushes from the river disappointment*, a Quebec Writers' Federation finalist for the A.M. Klein Prize for Poetry, the winner of *The Sixty-Four: Best Poets of 2018*, a recipient of the Sage Hill Writing award for Black Excellence, and a Canada Council of the Arts grantee. Her work has been critically praised and featured in well over one hundred periodicals and anthologies, in print and online, throughout Canada, the US, and Europe. She is a citizen of Canada, Panama, and the US, and has lived most of her life in Quebec.

Printed by Imprimerie Gauvin
Gatineau, Québec